Looking at Insects

David Glover

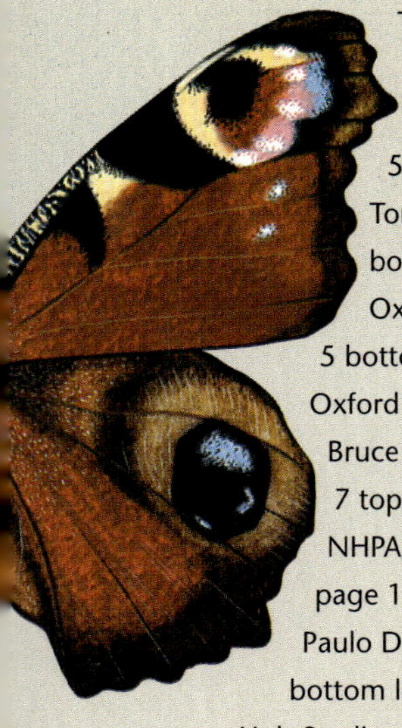

Photo Credits

Tony Stone Worldwide/David Higgs, page 5 top left.
Telegraph Colour Library/David Aubrey, page 5 top right.
Tony Stone Images/Christoph Burki, page 5 bottom left.
Oxford Scientific Films/James H Robinson, page 5 bottom right.
Oxford Scientific Films/J A L Cooke, page 7 top left.
Bruce Coleman Limited/Luiz Claudio Marigo, page 7 top right.
NHPA/Stephen Dalton, page 7 bottom left and page 11 top right.
Paulo De Oliveira, page 7 bottom right and page 9 bottom left.
Holt Studios International/Nigel Cattlin, page 9 top left and top right, page15 top left and page 17 top left.
Telegraph Colour Library/G Shumway, page 9 bottom right.
Science Photo Library/Claudio Nuridsany and Marie Perennou, page 11 top left, page 13 bottom left and page 21 top.
Telegraph Colour Library Masterfile, page 11 bottom left.
Science Photo Library/Dr M Read, page 11 bottom right.
NHPA/Michael Tweedie, page 13 top left and page 19 bottom right.
Telegraph Colour Library/Geof Du Feu, page 13 top right.
Planet Earth Pictures/Brian Kenney, page 13 bottom right.
Bruce Coleman Limited/Kim Taylor page 15 top right.
NHPA/G I Bernard, page 15 bottom left.
NHPA/Anthony Bannister page 15 bottom right.
Tony Stone Images/Tim Flach, page 17 top right.
Bruce Coleman Limited/Andy Purcell, page 17 bottom left, page 19 top right and page 20 top.
Science Photo Library/Noah Poritz, page 17 bottom right.
Science Photo Library/Dr J Burgess, page 19 top left.
Science Photo Library/Astrid and Hans-Frieder Michler, page 19 bottom left.
Tony Stone Images/Schafer and Hill, page 20 bottom.
Oxford Scientific Films/G I Bernard, page 21 bottom.

All Illustrations by Alan Male/Linden Artists

Discovery World:
Looking at Insects

a division of Reed Elsevier Inc.
500 Coventry Lane
Crystal Lake, IL 60014

02 01 00 99 98
10 9 8 7 6 5 4 3 2 1

Printed in the United States of America
ISBN 0-7635-2354-2

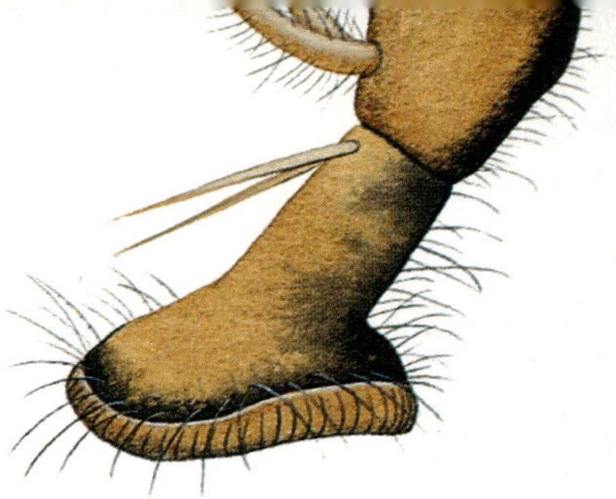

Contents

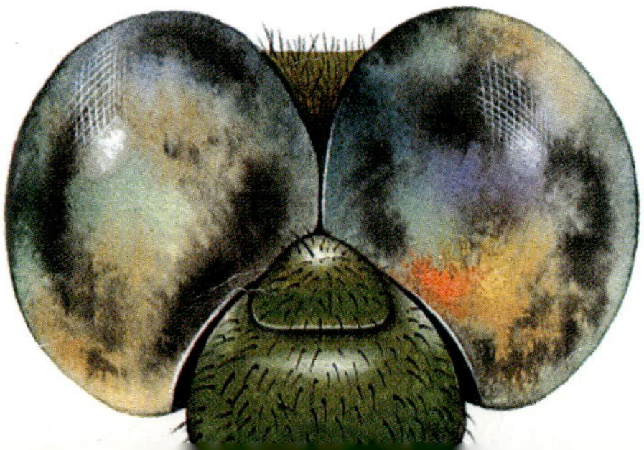

Rigby

Insects

Insects are small animals. They are different shapes and sizes. All insects have six legs and a body with three main parts. Some insects have wings. All insects have a mouth, eyes, and two antennae.

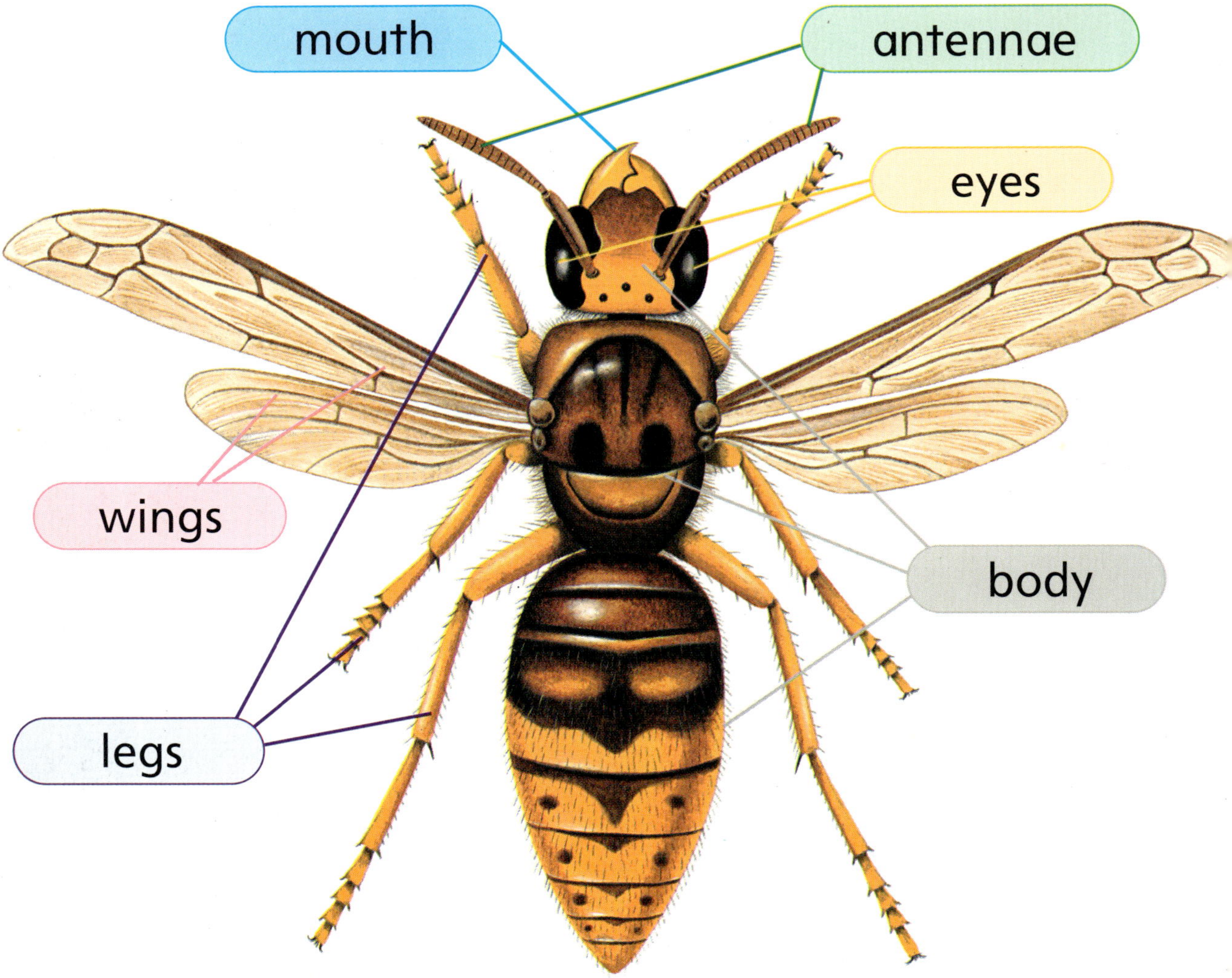

Which of these animals are insects?

1 beetle

2 crab

3 spider

4 housefly

Body

All insects have a body which is hard on the outside. They do not have bones.

Which insects do these bodies belong to?

1. long, smooth body for flying fast and straight

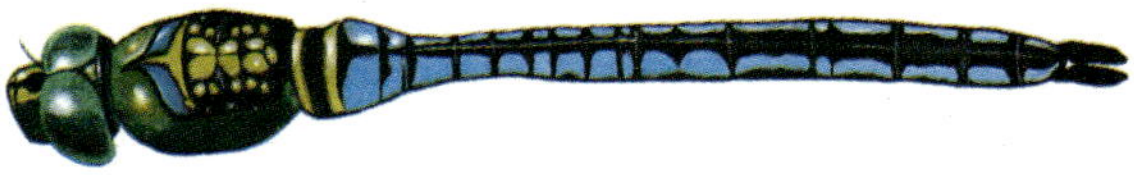

2. flat body for hiding on leaves

3. brightly colored body to warn birds not to eat it

4. thin body for hiding in twigs and leaves

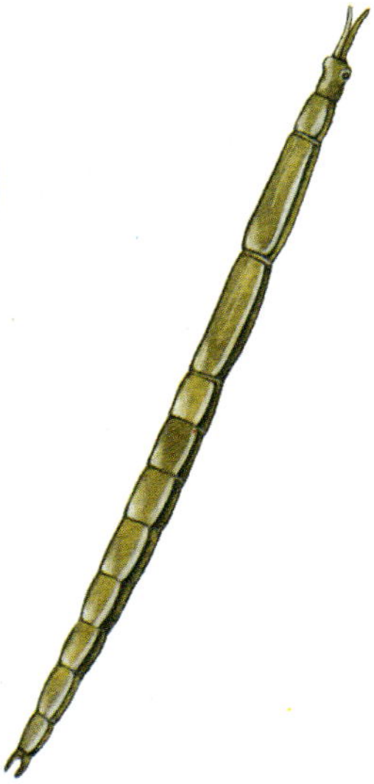

ladybug

walkingstick

dragonfly

leaf bug

Legs

All insects have six legs. The legs are fixed to the middle part of their bodies.

Which insects do these legs belong to?

1 back legs with hairs on them to collect pollen

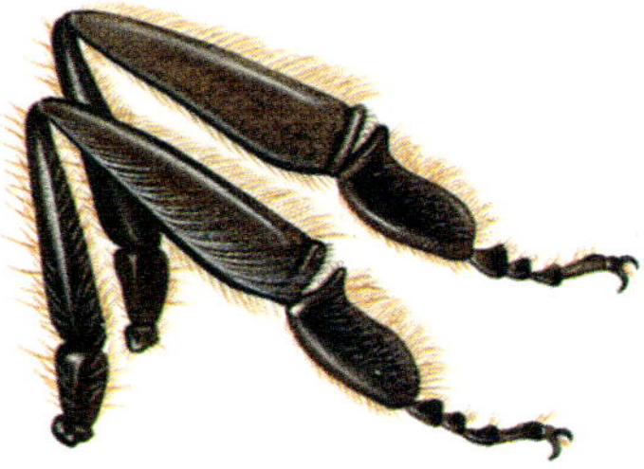

2 back legs which bend for swimming

3 back legs with strong muscles for jumping

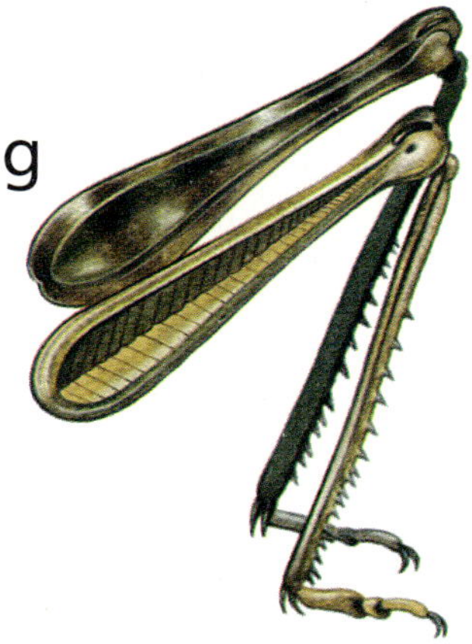

4 front legs with sharp spikes to help catch prey

grasshopper

honeybee

great diving beetle

praying mantis

Wings

Some insects have wings. Some insects have more than one pair of wings. There are some insects that have no wings at all.

Which insects do these wings belong to?

1 long, strong wings for flying fast

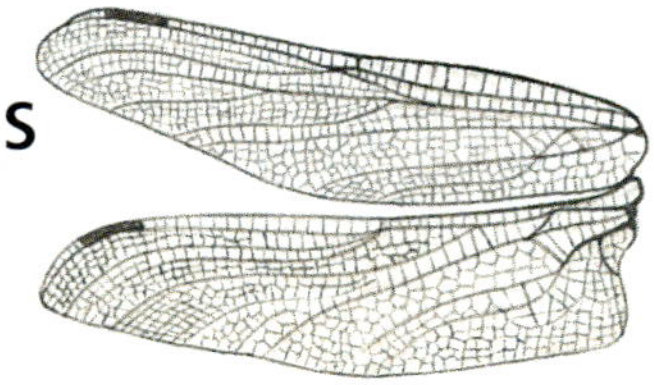

2 small wings to fly in and out of flowers

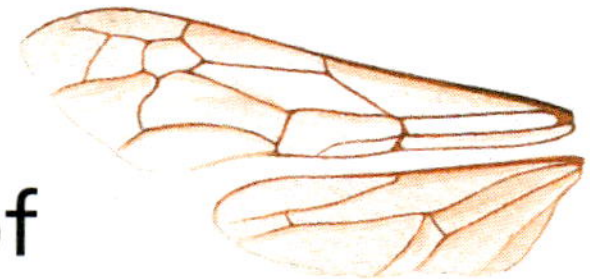

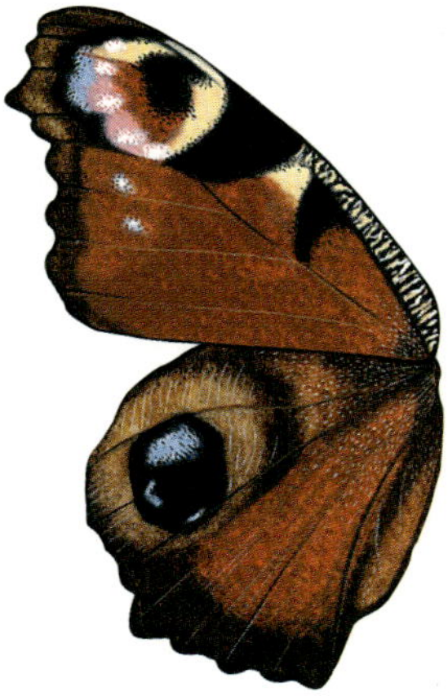

3 colorful wings to attract a mate

4 wings kept in wing cases for protection

ladybug

honeybee

dragonfly

butterfly

Mouth

All insects use their mouths for feeding. Some insects eat plants. Some insects are hunters and catch small animals for food. Some insects suck human blood.

Which insects do these mouths belong to?

1 strong jaws for chewing

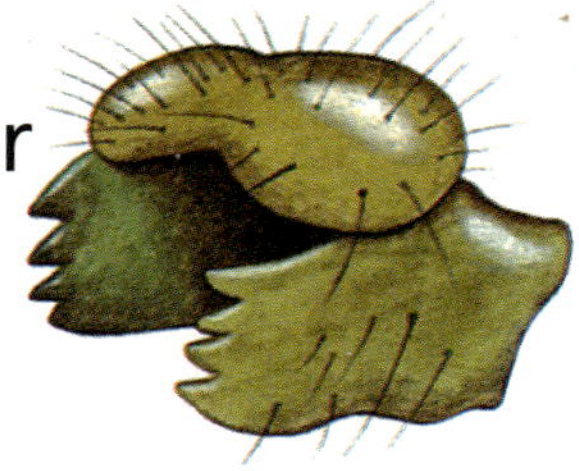

2 a long tube for sucking nectar

3 a sponge for soaking up food

4 a tube for sucking blood

★ *A caterpillar is the larva of a butterfly or moth.*

butterfly

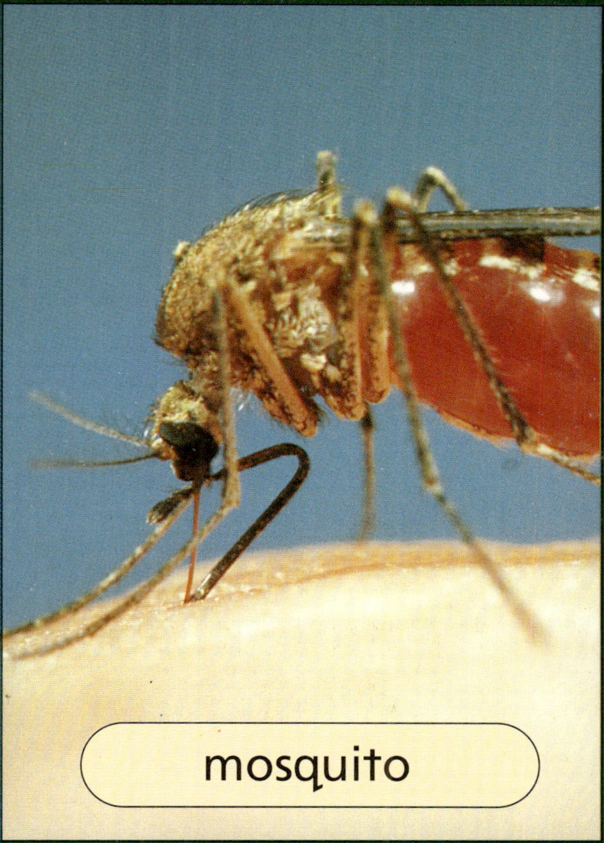

mosquito

housefly

★caterpillar

Eyes

Most insects have two large eyes. Their eyes are special. They can see in different directions at the same time.

Which insects do these eyes belong to?

1 large eyes at the sides of the head to see fast-moving prey

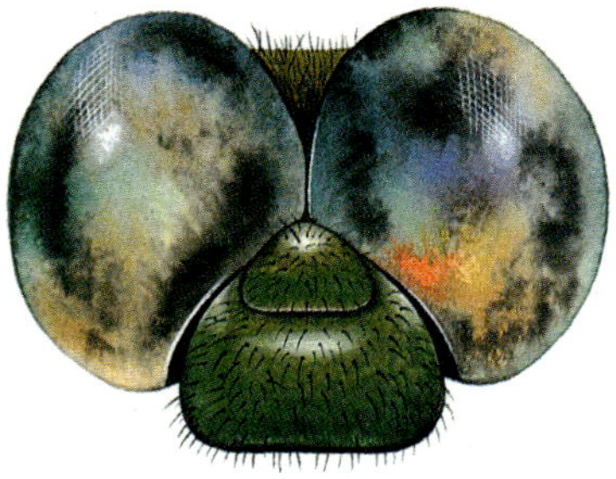

2 two pairs of eyes to see above and below water

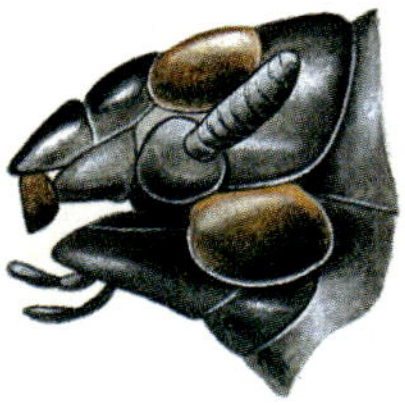

3 tiny eyes, as this insect finds its prey by smell and touch

4 eyes on the top of the head to watch for danger

housefly

dragonfly

flea

whirligig beetle

Antennae

All insects have two antennae. Antennae are long feelers. Some insects can smell and taste with their antennae.

Which insects do these antennae belong to?

1 long antennae to find food in cracks and dark places

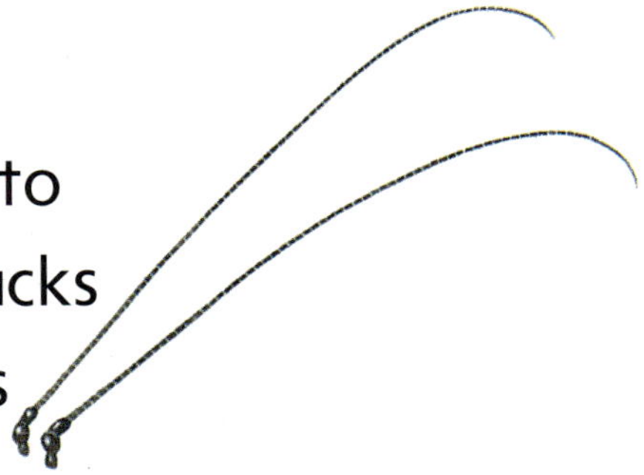

2 hairy antennae to smell people and other animals

3 feathery antennae to find a mate by smell

4 antennae to touch others

cockroach

ant

moth

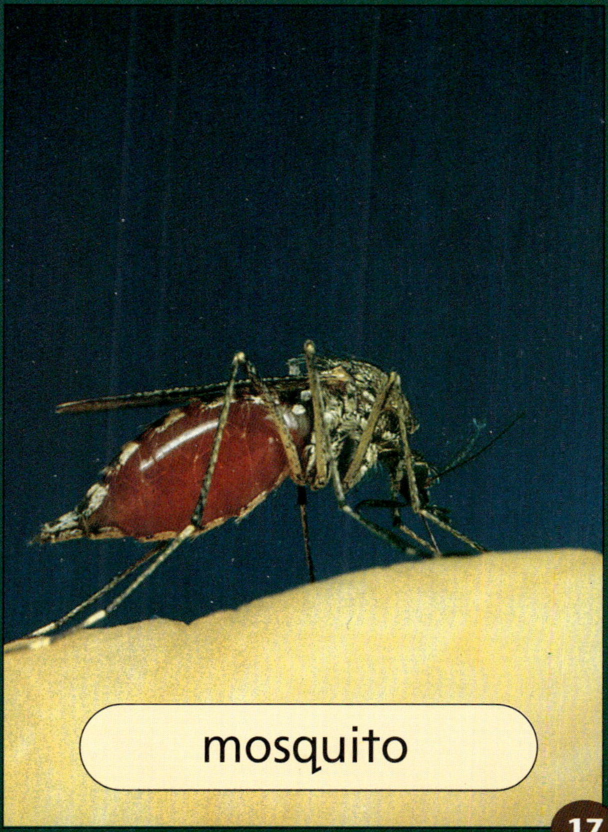

mosquito

Special Parts

Some insects have special parts at the ends of their bodies.

Which insects do these special parts belong to?

1. a stinger to attack enemies

2. a long tube for laying eggs

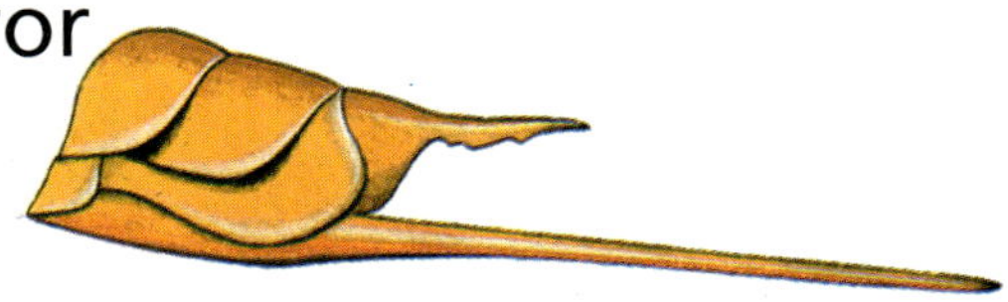

3. pincers to attack or bite enemies

4. a hole for squirting gas at enemies

honeybee

earwig

wood wasp

bombardier beetle

Insect Record Breakers

Goliath beetles are the heaviest insects in the world. They weigh about the same as a small candy bar.

Birdwing butterflies have the largest wings of any insect. Each wing is as big as a page of this book.

Giant walkingsticks are the longest insects in the world. They are nearly as long as your arm.

Cockroaches are the fastest running insects in the world. They can run as fast as you walk.

Answers

	1	2	3	4
Page 5	yes	no	no	yes
Page 6	dragonfly	leaf bug	ladybug	walking-stick
Page 8	honeybee	great diving beetle	grasshopper	praying mantis
Page 10	dragonfly	honeybee	butterfly	ladybug
Page 12	caterpillar	butterfly	housefly	mosquito
Page 14	dragonfly	whirligig beetle	flea	housefly
Page 16	cockroach	mosquito	moth	ant
Page 18	honeybee	wood wasp	earwig	bombardier beetle

Glossary

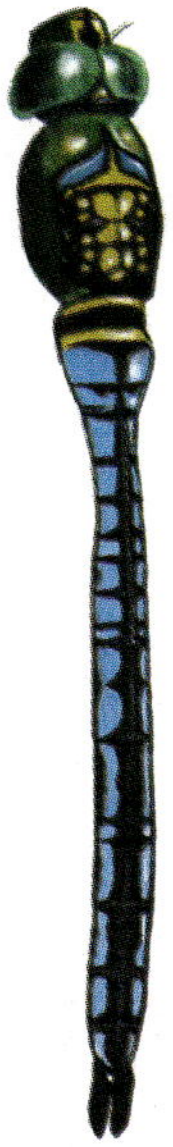

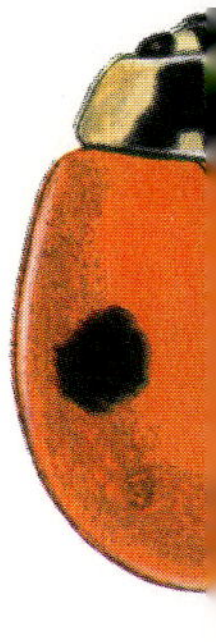

antennae
the two long feelers on an insect's head

larva
a stage in an insect's life before it becomes an adult

mate
one of a pair of male and female insects

nectar
a sweet juice made by flowers to attract insects

pollen
a fine powder inside a flower

wing cases
hard cases which protect the wings and bodies of insects

Index

a b c d e f g h i j k l m n o p q r s t u v w x y z